David M. Schwartz

MILLIONS TO MEASURE

by David M. Schwartz
pictures by Steven Kellogg

HarperCollins*Publishers*

There are millions of things—and many ways—to measure. Let's fly back in time and see how people measured many years ago.

When prehistoric people held a race, they had to think about distance.

They wanted to know about size and weight.

Traders had questions about volume.

A bright idea was needed.

And so people used their feet to measure distance.

It's one thousand feet to that rock!
READY! SET!

GO!

But measuring in feet could cause confusion . . .

You, my boy, are four feet tall.

My dad says I am four feet tall.

No way! I am three feet tall.

because feet come in different sizes.

To measure weight, people used stones.

But stones come in different sizes.

How many seeds could a container hold? That's one way volume was measured. But some seeds are tiny and others are huge, so once again measurements could mean mix-ups.

Time for another bright idea!

Let's fly forward in time!

Kings, queens, sultans, sheiks, and chiefs solved the problem of measuring with feet of different sizes. From now on, they declared, only one foot would be used throughout the land.

Foot-length rulers were made.

Standards were also set for weight and volume.

But what happened when people from faraway lands worked together? It was hard to decide which ruler's ruler would rule!

Gradually people began to use the same ruler, no matter who their ruler happened to be. Now a foot was a foot whether you lived in Eastonesia or Westlovakia.

Here is the kind of ruler we in the U.S. use today.

The green snake is one foot in length.

To measure something smaller than a foot, use inches. A foot is divided into twelve inches.

The pencil is three inches long.

No matter how I stretch and squirm, I still remain a half-inch worm.

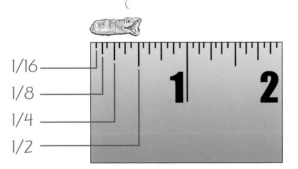

1/16
1/8
1/4
1/2

If you want to be very accurate, use fractions of an inch. You could measure to the half inch, quarter of an inch, and so on.

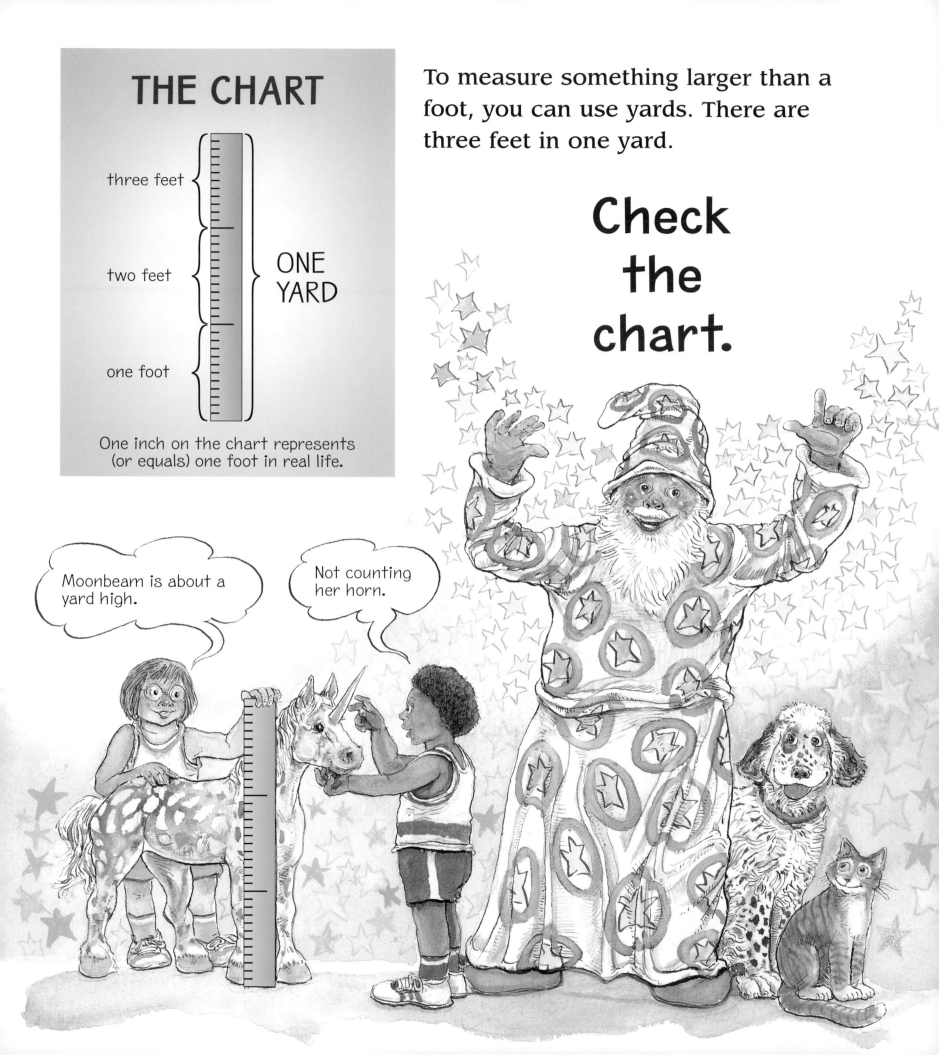

THE CHART

three feet

two feet

one foot

ONE YARD

One inch on the chart represents (or equals) one foot in real life.

To measure something larger than a foot, you can use yards. There are three feet in one yard.

Check the chart.

Moonbeam is about a yard high.

Not counting her horn.

We measure longer distances in miles. One mile is 5,280 feet. Mount Everest, the world's tallest peak, is about 29,000 feet . . . or 9,700 yards . . . or about 5 1/2 miles high.

Let's find out!

We usually measure weight in pounds. Jello weighs eight pounds. Robert weighs sixty-five pounds. So does Sandro.

However, if Sandro grows up to be an Olympic heavyweight wrestler, he might weigh 260 pounds.

But Sandro would be a pushover for Hercules the Huggable Hippo, whose weight is figured in tons. A ton is 2,000 pounds. Hercules weighs more than THREE TONS!

What if Sandro shrinks? If he dwindles to less than a pound, we would measure his weight in ounces. There are sixteen ounces in a pound. This bird weighs one ounce.

If we are weighing something even lighter, we would use fractions of an ounce. This spider weighs 1/10 of an ounce.

There are eight fluid ounces
in one cup.

There are two cups
in one pint.

There are two pints
in one quart.

There are four quarts
in one gallon.

Remember that cups were used to measure volume? We still use them to measure liquids.

Decide how thirsty you are; then check the chart.

Jello is happy with a fluid ounce of milk. But after his workout, Hercules has a humongous thirst. He'll guzzle gallons!

There are also smaller liquid measurements. There are two tablespoons in one fluid ounce. There are three teaspoons in a tablespoon. . . .

Hop back into the balloon! The bright idea we need dawned on a French priest in the late 1700s.

I've had enough of rulers and their rulers. We need a new system of measurement that is mathematically sound and logical! Check this out!

NEVER! NEVER! FEET FOREVER!

CONGRATULATIONS!

All of you ran a good race, and now you're probably thirsty. These water bottles each contain one liter. In the metric system liquid volume is measured in liters.

When the snail finally crosses the finish line, he'll probably be able to quench his thirst with a milliliter.

Running is a great way to shape up and lose weight. In the metric system we talk about losing (or gaining) mass. And mass is measured in grams.

Jello's mass is more impressive. She is over 3,600 grams.

Sandro and Robert both weigh 30 kilograms.

As Olympic wrestlers Sandro and Robert each weigh 118 kilograms. But they are no match for our champion, that truly massive and huggable hippo Hercules. He tips the scale at 3,000 kilograms. That's three metric tons!

Because the metric system is so logical and easy to use, it has been adopted by almost every country in the world. However, in the U.S. most people don't use the metric system.

As we have seen, confusion can result when people have different understandings about units of measure. And sometimes misunderstandings about measurements can lead to DISASTER!

The engineers and operators who worked on a multimillion-dollar spacecraft made a big mistake. Some of them used feet and miles, while others used meters and kilometers.

After blastoff the spacecraft

was supposed to orbit Mars, but instead it was lost in space forever.

Many people believe that the United States will eventually join the rest of the world and measure only in the metric system. But you don't have to wait until then, because you already know how!

Meters!

And liters!

And kilograms!

READY! SET! MEASURE!

Measuring and the Metric System

For many years, people in much of the world measured length and distance in a system that used inches, feet, yards, and miles, along with units that have disappeared completely, such as rods and leagues. They measured weight in ounces, pounds, and tons; and for volume they used fluid ounces, cups, pints, quarts, gallons, and barrels. This system used to be called the English system, but it is no longer used in England. It is sometimes called the inch-pound system, or the "customary system," even though it is customary in very few countries. Two of them are Liberia and Myanmar. One other, much bigger country uses it—the U.S.A. The rest of the world has found another way to measure. This can be confusing.

Remember the spacecraft that failed to orbit Mars? It's true! Investigators found that the people who built the *Mars Climate Observer* used English units. The operators used metric units. On September 23, 1999, the spacecraft was lost in space.

Another Way to Measure: The Metric System

In the late 1700s, the French people overthrew their king and queen. They established a democratically elected government. Some influential people in France didn't like the idea of using units that reminded them of the days when a monarch's body was the basis of measurements. They also wanted a measuring system that was based on scientific facts about our world. They invented something entirely new, superior to the old English system in many ways. People all over the world recognized how good it was, and it has spread to almost every country. This way of measuring is often called the metric system, but its official name is *Système International*, a French term meaning "International System." It is sometimes simply called SI.

The metric system is based on the meter (spelled *metre* in some countries). Originally, the meter was declared to be 1/10,000,000 of the distance between the North Pole and the equator. The meter has been redefined several times, and it is no longer exactly the same length as it was when it was invented in the 1790s.

Understanding Metric Units

One of the handiest things about the metric system is that if you learn just a few basic units and a few prefixes, you will understand all the units. In the same way that many words have prefixes (including the word *prefix*, which has the prefix *pre-*), so do metric measuring units. For example, *centi-* means "one-hundredth," so a centimeter is 1/100 of a meter. Another way to say that is that there are 100 centimeters in a meter. One of your fingers may be close to one centimeter across.

PREFIX	ABBREVIATION	MEANING		EXAMPLE	
kilo	k	one thousand	1000	kilometer	1000 meters
hecto	h	one hundred	100	hectometer	100 meters
deka	da	ten	10	dekameter	10 meters
deci	d	one-tenth	0.1	decimeter	0.1 meter
centi	c	one-hundredth	0.01	centimeter	0.01 meter
milli	m	one-thousandth	0.001	millimeter	0.001 meter

Metric units are usually written with abbreviations. It won't take you long to learn the abbreviations because there aren't many of them, and they always mean the same thing, no matter how they are being used. For instance, the abbreviation for *milli-* (meaning "one-thousandth") is a small *m* before the measurement that it refers to. So *milligram* is abbreviated *mg* because *g* is the abbreviation for *gram*. A milligram is 1/1000 of a gram. *Milliliter* is abbreviated *ml*, and *millimeter* is abbreviated *mm*. You get the idea.

There are other metric units that we have not used in this book. If you hear people talk about the weather anywhere outside the United States, you are likely to encounter temperatures measured in degrees Celsius (°C). As with other metric units, degrees Celsius are logical and simple to use. Water freezes at 0°C and boils at 100°C. (Compare that with degrees Fahrenheit, which are used in the United States. Water freezes at 32°F and boils at 212°F.)

You May Already Use the Metric System

Even though the metric system has not been adopted by people in the United States, many Americans use it every day. Look inside your refrigerator or kitchen cabinets. Juices, soft drinks, bottled waters, and other drinks sometimes come in containers labeled in liters, deciliters, or milliliters. Some kinds of dog food are labeled in kilograms. Now look in your medicine cabinet. Vitamins and medicines are almost always labeled in milligrams or grams. Some kinds of dental floss are measured in meters, and the volume of some brands of mouthwash is given in liters or milliliters. Shampoos, toothpastes, and hair sprays may also be labeled with metric measurements. Your family's car is probably measured in metric units. The parts of modern bicycles are usually sized in millimeters or centimeters. Many manufacturers use metric units because they are understood all over the world. Scientists and doctors always measure this way because the units are easy to use, and because they are understood by other scientists and doctors, no matter where they live.

The All-important Metric Number

Just like our number system, the metric system is based on the number 10. For example, there are 10 decimeters in a meter, 10 centimeters in a decimeter, and 10 millimeters in a centimeter. In most cases, each metric unit is ten times larger than the next smaller unit, and one-tenth as large as the next largest. (In some cases, the units are 1,000 times as large or small as the next ones, but that still means they are based on 10 because 1,000 is 10 x 10 x 10.) The customary system is not based on anything in particular. There are 12 inches in a foot, 3 feet in a yard, and 5,280 feet (or 1,760 yards) in a mile. No one would call that a user-friendly way to measure! Using a number system and a measuring system that do not work together is like trying to get two people who speak different languages to communicate. It can be done, but it's not easy.

If you want to see how much easier it is to work with the metric system, try to multiply your height in centimeters by any amount (say 40); then multiply your height in feet and inches by the same amount. You can even use a calculator if you want to. Which system is easier to use?

The Most Amazing Thing of All About the Metric System

Units are related to one another even if they measure completely different things. There's a connection between the units of length, mass, volume, and temperature. If you very carefully measure one milliliter of water with very precise equipment, and pour it into a cube, the cube would be exactly 1 cm long X 1cm wide X 1 cm high at 4° Celsius. Another way to describe that cube is to say it's "one cubic centimeter" (or 1cc, for short). So, you can see that there's a connection between volume (milliliters) and length (centimeters). But there's more: One cubic centimeter of water has a mass of exactly one gram at 4° Celsius. So in the metric system, measurements of length, volume, and mass are all related to one another, and to the most important liquid in our lives.

Think Metric!

We don't recommend you change metric measurements into customary measurements, or vice versa. When you are starting to use metric measurements, you will be tempted to convert centimeters to inches or kilograms to pounds or degrees Celsius to degrees Fahrenheit. But if you convert back and forth between the two systems, you will have a much harder time learning the metric system. Learning a measuring system is a little like learning a language (but much easier). Babies learn their native tongue because they are immersed in it. When you were younger, it didn't take you long to learn the words *ice cream*. You heard the words, you swallowed the delicious cold stuff, and you remembered the meaning of those two words. It's the same with learning to measure in a new system. Use metric units every day. Find out how tall you are in centimeters, how much you weigh (your mass, actually) in kilograms, how much milk your family drinks in liters, the distance to your school in kilometers, the temperature every day in degrees Celsius, and so on. Once you start measuring and thinking this way, you'll soon learn the metric system. You'll be measuring like a world citizen.

To Paul and Leah,

cousins beyond measure

—D.M.S.

Love to the GREAT GREENS:

Courtney, Lachlan, Nathan, Sally, and Bob

—S.K.

Millions to Measure

Text copyright © 2003 by David M. Schwartz   Illustrations copyright © 2003 by Steven Kellogg

Library of Congress Cataloging-in-Publication Data

Schwartz, David M.

  Millions to measure / by David M. Schwartz ; pictures by Steven Kellogg.

  p.   cm.

  Summary: Marvelosissimo the Magician explains the development of standard units of measure,
and shows the simplicity of calculating length, height, weight, and volume using the metric system.

  ISBN-10: 0-688-12916-1 (trade bdg.) — ISBN-13: 978-0-688-12916-3 (trade bdg.)

  ISBN-10: 0-06-623784-X (lib. bdg.) — ISBN-13: 978-0-06-623784-8 (lib. bdg.)

  ISBN-10: 0-06-084806-5 (pbk.) — ISBN-13: 978-0-06-084806-4 (pbk.)

  1. Mensuration—Juvenile literature.   [1. Measurement.   2. Weights and measures.

3. Metric system.]   I. Kellogg, Steven.   II. Title.

QA465 .S315   2003   530.8—dc21   2001039683

Typography by Matt Adamec